The Ultimate "WHY" Book

for Curious Kids

Vol. 1 - The Sky

Fun Science Facts and How Things Work Explained with Simple Analogies in 5 Minutes or Less

LILO LU

Preface

Welcome to The Ultimate WHY Book for Curious Kids!

When I was a small kid, I was always curious about how the world works. I would ask endless questions, trying to understand the wonders around me. Now that I'm older, I see the same curiosity in my kids. They're always asking questions too, wanting to know how things happen, why they happen, and what makes our world so amazing.

That's why I created this book—just for curious minds like yours! **The Ultimate WHY Book** is filled with the questions that kids always want to ask, explained in a fun and engaging way that's easy to understand. Whether you're wondering how rainbows form, why the sky is blue, or how animals know where to go, this book has the answers, and it's designed to make learning exciting!

And guess what? There's also a special edition just for parents! The parent's edition is meant to be read alongside this book and serves as a guide to explain things in a little more detail. It's like having a secret key to understanding the world together!

So, let's dive into the wonders of our world and start exploring all the "whys" that make life so interesting. Who knows? Maybe you'll discover new questions along the way!

To Leanne,

may your life be filled with wonder, joy and endless exploration!

Contents

This book belongs to

Why is the sky blue?

a) The sky is blue because the ocean reflects its colour.
b) The sky is blue because the blue fairy has spread its fairy dust all over the sky.
c) The sky is blue because of the way sunlight interacts with Earth's atmosphere.

Explanation:
Imagine sunlight as a big box of crayons with colors like red, orange, yellow, green, blue, and purple. When sunlight comes down from the sky, it's like a bunch of these crayons all mixed together, making white light.

Here's the fun part! The air around us is like a ***big*** party with many tiny, invisible balloons. When the sunlight comes through, it bumps into these tiny balloons. The blue crayon light has shorter, smaller waves, so it's really good at bouncing off these balloons and spreading them all over the place.

It's like if you were playing with a blue balloon and shined a flashlight on it. The blue light would bounce around the room and make everything look blue. That's what happens in the sky! The blue light from the sun bounces around the air, making the whole sky look blue to us.

So, the sky is blue because the blue light from the sun gets bounced all over the place by tiny balloons in the air. Cool, right?

Interesting Fact: The sky on Earth isn't always blue! On Mars, the sky often appears a dusty yellow or reddish-pink due to the fine particles of rust-colored dust in its atmosphere. However, the Martian sky can take on a blueish hue during sunrise and sunset. This is because the dust particles scatter the red light, letting more blue light through, similar to how Earth's sky appears blue during the day!

Correct answer: c) The sky is blue because of the way sunlight interacts with Earth's atmosphere.

Bonus Experiment: Make Your Own Blue Sky in a Jar

What You'll Need:

- A clear glass jar or a large, clear glass cup
- Water
- A few drops of milk or a small amount of powdered milk
- A flashlight (a phone flashlight works too!)
- A dark room or a space where you can dim the lights

Steps:

1. Fill the Jar: Fill the glass jar or cup almost to the top with water.

2. Add the Milk: Add just a few drops of milk into the water and stir it gently. The water should become slightly cloudy, like a misty sky.

3. Find a Dark Spot: Take the jar to a room where you can dim or turn the lights off. This will make it easier to see the effect.

4. Shine the Light: Turn on your flashlight and shine it through the side of the jar, not from the top. Watch closely! The light passing through the cloudy water should start to look a little bluish, just like the sky.

5. Observe and Explain: Notice how the water appears bluish where the light passes through? That's because the tiny milk particles in the water scatter the blue light from the flashlight, just like the air molecules scatter blue light from the sun in our sky.

6. Extra Fun: If you shine the light through the jar at an angle, you might see the light on the other side looking a bit red or orange, similar to how the sky looks during sunrise or sunset.

What's Happening?

The milk particles in the water are like the air molecules in the sky. When light passes through, the blue part of the light gets scattered more, making the water look blue. This is similar to why the sky looks blue during the day!

Safety Note: Handle the flashlight and glass jar carefully. Always ask an adult for help when needed!

POP QUIZ

1. What happens when sunlight comes down from the sky?

a) It turns into one color

b) It splits into lots of colors, like a big box of crayons

c) It only shows blue

2. Why does the sky look blue?

a) Because the blue light from the sun gets bounced around by tiny balloons in the air

b) Because red light bounces all over the place

c) Because the sun is blue

3. What do the tiny balloons in the air do to the sunlight?

a) They make the sunlight disappear

b) They turn the sunlight into rainbows

c) They bounce the blue light all over, making the sky look blue

Color the sky blue!

Answer: B, A, C

Why do clouds form?

a) Clouds form when warm air rises, cools down, and the water vapor in it condenses into tiny droplets.
b) Clouds form when the sky is stretching.
c) Clouds form when air pressure pushes water from the oceans into the sky.

Explanation:

Think about when you take a hot shower, and the bathroom fills with steam. This steam is water vapor, which is water in its gas form. Clouds form in a similar way, but up in the sky.

When the sun heats the ground, it warms up the air near the surface. Warm air rises because it is lighter than cool air. As the warm air rises higher into the sky, it starts to cool down. Cooler air can't hold as much water vapor as warm air can, so the water vapor starts to condense or turn back into tiny water droplets.

These tiny water droplets stick together to form clouds. It's like when you see your breath on a cold day—your warm breath turns into tiny droplets you can see in the air. Millions of tiny droplets come together in the sky to form a cloud.

So, clouds are made up of tiny water droplets or sometimes even ice crystals. They form when warm air rises, cools down, and the water vapor in the air changes back into liquid form. This warm air rising and cooling process is why we see clouds floating in the sky. It's like nature's way of making fluffy, floating water!

Interesting Fact: Did you know that even though clouds look light and fluffy, they can weigh as much as 100 elephants? Water droplets stay up in the sky because they are small and spread out, making them lighter than the air around them, allowing them to float.

Correct Answer: a) Clouds form when warm air rises, cools down, and the water vapor in it condenses into tiny droplets.

Bonus Experiment: Create a Cloud in a Jar

What You'll Need:

- A clear glass jar with a lid
- Hot water (ask an adult for help!)
- Ice cubes
- A small plate or saucer
- Hairspray or aerosol air freshener (optional, and use with adult supervision)

Steps:

1. Heat the Water: With the help of an adult, pour about 1-2 inches of hot water into the jar. The water should be steaming but not boiling.

2. Create a Cold Lid: Place the small plate or saucer upside down on top of the jar. Then, put a few ice cubes on top of the plate. This will cool the air inside the jar.

3. Wait and Watch: Let the jar sit for a minute or two. You'll start to see some condensation forming inside the jar, which looks like mist.

4. Add the Hairspray (Optional): If you want to make the cloud more visible, quickly lift the plate, spray a tiny amount of hairspray or aerosol air freshener into the jar, and immediately put the plate with the ice cubes back on top.

5. See the Cloud: After a few seconds, you should see a cloud form inside the jar! The cloud is made of tiny water droplets, just like real clouds in the sky.

6. Release the Cloud: You can remove the plate and let the "cloud" escape into the air.

What's Happening?

This experiment shows how clouds form. The hot water in the jar creates warm, moist air. When the warm air rises and hits the cold lid (which is like the cool upper atmosphere), it cools down. As it cools, the water vapor in the air condenses into tiny droplets, forming a cloud. The hairspray or air freshener helps by giving the water vapor something to cling to, making the cloud more visible.

Safety Note: Make sure to do this experiment with an adult, especially when handling hot water.

Why is the cloud white?

a) Clouds are white because they reflect all the colors of sunlight equally.
b) Clouds are white because they are filled with snowflakes that reflect sunlight.
c) Clouds are white because they are made of tiny ice crystals that scatter blue light.

Explanation:

Imagine you have a flashlight that shines many colors of light, like a rainbow. When this light hits the tiny water droplets and ice crystals in the cloud, all those colors mix together and bounce off in every direction. When all the colors of the rainbow mix together, they make white light! That's why clouds look white to us.

Now, think of the sunlight as being made of all those colors, even though it looks white to us. When sunlight shines on a cloud, the tiny water droplets and ice crystals reflect all the colors of the sunlight equally, the cloud looks white to us, just like when you mix all your crayons together!

It's kind of like when you shine a flashlight on a white piece of paper. The paper doesn't just show one color—it reflects all the light back, making it look white. The same thing happens with clouds in the sky. The sunlight hits the cloud, and because the cloud reflects all the light back equally, it appears white.

Sometimes, clouds can look gray or dark if they get really thick or if there's a lot of water inside them. When this happens, the sunlight has a harder time getting through, making the cloud look darker. But when the cloud is light and fluffy, it reflects the sun's light perfectly, making it look bright and white.

Interesting Fact: Did you know that the same reason clouds are white is why snow looks white too? Snowflakes are made of ice crystals, just like some of the tiny particles in clouds, and they reflect all the colors of light, making them appear white!

Correct answer: a) Clouds are white because they reflect all the colors of sunlight equally.

Can I touch the sky if I go really high?

a) Yes, you can touch the sky if you go high enough in an airplane or a rocket.
b) No, you can't touch the sky because the sky is not a solid thing you can reach.
c) Maybe, but only if you climb the tallest mountain in the world.

Explanation:

Looking up, it seems like the sky is this big, blue thing way up high. But the sky isn't solid like a wall or the ground; it's actually made of air, which is everywhere around us, even though we can't see it. The blue color we see is because of how sunlight scatters in the air, but it doesn't mean the sky is something you can touch.

When we're outside, we're already in the sky, surrounded by air! As you go higher and higher, like in an airplane or a rocket, the air gets thinner, but you still won't find a spot where the sky ends. The "sky" is just the space above Earth where air and clouds float.

Imagine you're blowing bubbles. The bubbles float around and look like they're part of the sky. But if you try to grab one, it pops, and you can't really hold onto it. The sky is kind of like that. Even if you go really high in a plane or a hot air balloon, you're still moving through the air, and there's nothing to grab or touch.

So, no matter how high you go, whether you're on a mountain or in an airplane, you won't be able to touch the sky. But don't worry, it's still fun to look up at the clouds, birds, and stars that live in the sky!

Interesting Fact: Did you know that airplanes fly so high in the sky that the air becomes really thin, and the sky starts to look darker, almost like it's turning into space?

Correct answer: b) No, the sky isn't something you can touch because it's just the air all around us.

POP QUIZ

1. What happens to warm air when it rises higher into the sky?

a) It cools down and the water vapor turns into tiny water droplets

b) It disappears

c) It stays the same and forms rain right away

2. Why do clouds look white?

a) Because they are filled with snow

b) Because all the colors of light mix together and make white light

c) Because they reflect the blue sky

3. What are clouds made of?

a) Tiny water droplets or ice crystals

b) Cotton balls

c) Air bubbles

How many clouds can you count?

Answer: a, b, a

Why do rainbows appear?

a) Rainbows appear because the sun's rays are bent and split into different colors by raindrops.
b) Rainbows appear because clouds mix different colors in the sky after it rains.
c) Rainbows appear because the birds color the sky with crayons.

Explanation:

Imagine you have a glass prism, a special piece of glass that can split light into different colors. When you shine a flashlight through it, you see a rainbow. Something similar happens in the sky when it rains and the sun is shining.

Raindrops act like tiny prisms. When sunlight enters a raindrop, it bends, or changes direction, because of the water. Inside the raindrop, the light splits into different colors: red, orange, yellow, green, blue, indigo, and violet. These are the colors of the rainbow. The light then bends again when it leaves the raindrop.

Because millions of raindrops do this simultaneously, all the colors spread out in a big circle, creating a rainbow in the sky. This bending and splitting of sunlight by raindrops is why we see rainbows.

So, next time you see a rainbow, you'll know it's because sunlight is bending and splitting into different colors as it passes through raindrops. It's nature's way of showing the hidden colors in sunlight, making the sky look magical!

Interesting Fact: Did you know that every person sees their own personal rainbow? That's because the appearance of a rainbow depends on where you're standing and where the sun is in the sky. So, if you and a friend are looking at a rainbow, you're actually seeing two different rainbows!

Correct answer: a) Rainbows appear because the sun's rays are bent and split into different colors by raindrops.

Bonus Experiment: Create Your Own Rainbow

What You'll Need:

- A glass of water (clear glass)
- A small mirror
- A flashlight or sunlight
- A white piece of paper

Steps:

1. Set Up: Fill the glass with water almost to the top. Place the small mirror inside the glass at an angle so that part of it is submerged in the water and part is above it.

2. Find the Light: Take the glass with the mirror and place it near a window where sunlight is shining through, or use a flashlight. Make sure the light is shining directly onto the mirror inside the water.

3. Catch the Rainbow: Hold the white piece of paper so it's in the path of the light that reflects off the mirror. Adjust the angle of the paper and the mirror until you see a rainbow appear on the paper!

What's happening?

The rainbow appears because the light bends (refracts) when it moves from air into the water. The mirror reflects the light, splitting it into the colors of the rainbow—just like how rainbows form in the sky after it rains!

This experiment shows that white light is made up of many colors, and you can see them all by making your very own rainbow. Have fun exploring the colors and trying different angles to make your rainbow bigger, brighter, and more exciting!

Why can't I see rainbow at night?

a) Rainbows only appear during the day because they need sunlight to form.
b) Rainbows are shy and only come out when the moon is full.
c) Rainbows hide at night because they don't like the dark.

Explanation:

Rainbows only appear during the day because they need sunlight to form. A rainbow happens when sunlight passes through raindrops in the sky. The light gets bent and split into different colors, creating the beautiful arc we see. But at night, the sun isn't out, so there's no sunlight to make a rainbow. Without sunlight, the raindrops can't bend the light, and that's why we don't see rainbows at night.

However, there's something cool called a "moonbow," which is like a rainbow but made by the light of the moon. Moonbows are much fainter and harder to see because moonlight isn't as bright as sunlight, but they can still happen!

Moonbows are much rarer than daytime rainbows because they require specific conditions: a full or nearly full moon, clear skies, and moisture in the air, such as from rain or mist. Since moonlight is much fainter than sunlight, moonbows often appear white to the human eye, although long-exposure photography can reveal the full spectrum of colors. Moonbows are commonly seen near waterfalls or in areas with frequent showers, like Hawaii or the Cumberland Falls in Kentucky, USA.

Interesting Fact: Did you know that rainbows are actually full circles? We usually only see the top half because the ground gets in the way, but if you were up high in the sky, like in an airplane, you might see a full circular rainbow!

Correct answer: a) Rainbows only appear during the day because they need sunlight to form.

What happens if you find the end of a rainbow?

a) If you find the end of a rainbow, you'll discover a pot of gold hidden by leprechauns.

b) The end of a rainbow is just an illusion, so you can never actually reach it.

c) When you find the end of a rainbow, it disappears because rainbows are magical.

Explanation:

The end of a rainbow is just an illusion, which means it isn't a real place you can reach. A rainbow forms when sunlight shines through raindrops in the sky, bending and splitting the light into different colors. This creates a beautiful arc of colors that we see in the sky.

Here's the trick: a rainbow doesn't actually have a real "end" because it's made of light. As you move closer to what looks like the end of the rainbow, it will keep moving away from you! That's why no matter how far you walk or drive, you can never reach the end of a rainbow. It's like chasing a shadow—no matter how fast you run, you can't catch it.

Rainbows are just one of nature's amazing tricks, and that's what makes them so magical to see.

Interesting Fact: Did you know that Hawaii is often considered the place with the most rainbows in the world? Due to its unique climate, frequent rain showers, and ample sunshine, Hawaii provides ideal conditions for rainbow formation. The combination of tropical weather patterns and the islands' mountainous terrain creates numerous opportunities for rainbows to appear, sometimes even double or triple rainbows. As a result, Honolulu is also known as "The Rainbow State."

Correct answer: b) The end of a rainbow is just an illusion, so you can never actually reach it.

POP QUIZ

1. What acts like tiny prisms in the sky to create a rainbow?

a) Clouds

b) The sun

c) Raindrops

2. Why don't we see rainbows at night?

a) Because there are no raindrops at night

b) Because there's no sunlight to make a rainbow

c) Because the moonlight is too strong

3. Why can't you reach the end of a rainbow?

a) Because it's just an illusion made of light, and it moves as you move

b) Because it's always too far away

c) Because it's hidden behind the clouds

Color the rainbow

Answer: c, b, a

Why does the sun follow me?

a) The sun follows you because it's connected to your shadow.
b) The sun follows you because it likes you.
c) The sun seems to follow you because it's so far away that it looks like it's in the same spot no matter where you go.

Explanation:

Have you ever noticed that the sun seems to follow you everywhere you go when you're outside? It might feel like it's keeping an eye on you, but the truth is a little different! The sun is actually super far away from us—about 93 million miles away! That's so far that even if you run as fast as you can or even drive across the country, the sun will still look like it's in the same spot in the sky.

Think about a giant ball in the sky that's so far away that no matter how much you move around, it looks like it's always right there above you. That's because the sun is so big and far away from where you're standing that it doesn't change position much when you move around on Earth. This is why it seems like the sun is following you, even though it's just staying in the same place, shining down on everyone all at once.

So, the next time you're outside, and it feels like the sun is following you, remember that it's just far away and shining over the whole world, making it look like it's moving with you!

Interesting Fact: Did you know that it takes about 8 minutes and 20 seconds for sunlight to reach Earth? That means when you see the sun, you're actually looking at it as it was over 8 minutes ago!

Correct answer: c) The sun seems to follow you because it's so far away that it looks like it's in the same spot no matter where you go.

Observation Activity: Why Does the Sun Follow Me?

Objective: To help kids understand why the sun appears to follow them when they're walking, driving, or moving around.

What You'll Need:

- A sunny day
- An open area outside where the sun is visible
- A small object, like a toy or a ball
- An adult to join you

Steps:

1. Go Outside: Find a spot where you can clearly see the sun in the sky. Make sure it's a safe place to observe the sun without staring directly at it (remind kids to never look directly at the sun).

2. Start Moving: Walk around in a straight line or move in a circle. Notice that as you move, the sun seems to stay in the same spot in the sky and doesn't appear to move or change position. It almost looks like it's following you!

3. Observe the Toy or Ball: Hold a small toy or ball in your hand and stretch your arm out in front of you. As you walk around, notice how the toy or ball seems to move with you. Even though you're moving, the toy stays in the same position relative to you. The sun works in a similar way!

What's Happening?

The sun appears to follow you because it is incredibly far away from Earth. No matter how much you move, your position relative to the sun doesn't change enough for you to notice any difference in its position in the sky. This is why it seems like the sun is always in the same place, following you as you move.

Why is the sun so hot?

a) The sun is so hot because it's made of burning coal like a giant campfire.
b) The sun is so hot because it's closer to Earth than any other star.
c) The sun is so hot because it's a big ball of gas where tiny particles smash together and release a lot of energy.

Explanation:

Imagine you have a campfire. You know how it gets really hot when the fire burns? Now imagine a fire that's way, way more significant than any campfire you've ever seen—so big that it's like millions of campfires all burning together! The sun is like that, except it isn't made of wood or coal like a normal fire. Instead, the sun comprises two special gases called hydrogen and helium.

Here's how it works: The sun constantly has tiny explosions inside it, a bit like a fireworks show that never stops! These explosions are called "**nuclear fusion**." They happen when the sun smashes hydrogen atoms together to make helium, and this process releases a lot of energy, which we feel as heat and light. So, the sun isn't burning like a campfire; instead, it's like a super-powered energy machine!

It's like blowing up a balloon. When you push air into the balloon, it gets bigger. The sun pushes gas together so hard and fast that it creates powerful explosions, which is why it gets so hot. All that heat then travels through space and reaches Earth, warming us up.

Even though the sun is 93 million miles away, it's so big and powerful that we can still feel its heat on our skin when we step outside on a sunny day.

Interesting Fact: Did you know that the temperature at the sun's core is about 27 million degrees Fahrenheit (15 million degrees Celsius)? That's way hotter than any oven or fire on Earth!

Correct answer: c) The sun is so hot because it's a big ball of gas where tiny particles smash together and release a lot of energy.

Unlock the Power of Sharing Knowledge

"The best way to find yourself is to lose yourself in the service of others." - Mahatma Gandhi

Did you know that sharing what you know can brighten someone else's world, just like when sunlight makes clouds look white? It's true! By sharing, we make things better for everyone, and here's your chance to do just that.

Would you help someone just like you—curious about how the world works, but unsure where to start?

My mission with *The Ultimate WHY Book for Curious Kids* is to make understanding the big questions, like "Why is the sky blue?" or "Why do clouds form?", easy and fun for all kids (and maybe even grown-ups too!). I want every child to feel like a super scientist, discovering the wonders of the world around them.

But, to reach more curious minds, I need your help.

Most people pick books based on reviews, just like you might have done. That's why I'm asking you to help other kids and families who are eager to learn more about nature's coolest mysteries by leaving a review.

It doesn't cost anything and takes less than a minute, but your words could inspire someone to grab this book and go on their own journey of discovery. With your review, you could help...

...one more child get excited about science.
...one more parent find the perfect bedtime book.
...one more teacher share fun lessons in the classroom.
...one more kid explore experiments and ask "why" every day.

Want to make a difference? It's simple! Just scan the QR code below and leave your thoughts about *The Ultimate WHY Book for Curious Kids*. It can be just a few sentences, but it could spark a world of curiosity in others.

If you love helping others learn and explore, then you're exactly the kind of person I want to thank—so thank you, from the bottom of my heart!

With gratitude,
Lilo Lu

Why can't I look at the sun?

a) You can't look at the sun because it might make you feel too warm.
b) You can't look at the sun because it's so bright that it can hurt your eyes.
c) You can't look at the sun because it moves too fast across the sky.

Explanation:

Imagine you have a flashlight, and you turn it on at night. If you shine it right into your eyes, it feels too bright and might make you squint or close your eyes, right? Now, think of the sun as the world's biggest flashlight—except it's way, way brighter than any flashlight you've ever seen. The light from the sun is so powerful that it can hurt your eyes if you try to look at it directly.

When the sun's bright light enters your eyes, it can damage a part of your eye called the **retina**, which is like the camera inside your eye that helps you see. The retina is very sensitive, kind of like a delicate piece of paper that can get burned if you shine too much light on it. Even though you might not feel the pain right away, staring at the sun for too long can damage your vision and make it harder to see things clearly.

So remember, the sun is amazing, but it's best to enjoy it without looking right at it. You can still have fun outside in the sunshine; just make sure to keep your eyes safe!

Interesting Fact: Did you know that during a solar eclipse, when the moon covers the sun, it's the only time you might safely look at the sun, but only with special glasses that protect your eyes? The reduced light can trick your eyes into thinking it's safe to look directly at the sun, but the concentrated sunlight during an eclipse can cause even more severe damage to the retina. Always use solar or indirect viewing glasses to observe a solar eclipse safely!

Correct answer: b) You can't look at the sun because it's so bright that it can hurt your eyes.

Why does the sun look like it's being covered up?

a) The sun looks like it's being covered up because an eclipse happens when the moon turns into a giant cookie in the sky.
b) The sun looks like it's being covered up because the moon, Earth, or sun play a game of hide and seek, causing one to temporarily disappear.
c) The sun looks like it's being covered up because it's a magical event where stars decide to take a day off.

Explanation:

Picture this: you're playing hide-and-seek with your friends. Sometimes, you hide, and they seek, and other times, they hide, and you seek. An eclipse is a bit like a cosmic game of hide-and-seek. It happens when the sun, moon, and Earth line up in a straight line.

There are two main types of eclipses - **solar** and **lunar**. In a solar eclipse, the moon moves between the sun and the Earth, and it looks like the sun is hiding behind the moon. It's as if the sun is saying, "You can't find me!" But remember, never look directly at a solar eclipse without special glasses because the sun's rays can hurt your eyes.

In a lunar eclipse, the Earth moves between the sun and the moon, and the moon seems to disappear or change colour. It's like the moon is the one hiding this time.

So, an eclipse isn't about the moon turning into a giant cookie or stars taking a day off. It's a fascinating hide-and-seek game played by the sun, moon, and Earth. Isn't that a fun way to think about it?

Interesting Fact: Did you know that the longest a total solar eclipse can last is 7.5 minutes? That's a pretty short game of hide-and-seek between the sun and the moon!

Correct Answer: b) The sun looks like it's being covered up because the moon, Earth, or sun play a game of hide and seek, causing one to temporarily disappear.

Bonus Experiment: Create Your Own Eclipse at Home!

What You'll Need:

- A flashlight (this will be the sun)
- A small ball (like a ping-pong ball, this will be the moon)
- A larger ball (like a basketball, this will be the Earth)
- A dark room

Steps:

1. Set Up the Sun: Turn on the flashlight and place it on a table or have someone hold it steady. This will represent the sun shining its light across the room.

2. Position the Earth: Hold the larger ball (the Earth) about a foot away from the flashlight. Make sure the ball is between the flashlight (the sun) and where you'll be standing.

3. Create the Eclipse: Now, take the smaller ball (the moon) and slowly move it in front of the larger ball (the Earth). Watch as the shadow of the small ball (the moon) starts to cover the larger ball (the Earth). This is like what happens during an eclipse!

4. Watch the Eclipse: Keep moving the small ball until it completely covers the light shining on the larger ball. You've just created a solar eclipse! The small ball (moon) blocks the light from the flashlight (sun), creating a shadow on the larger ball (Earth).

What's happening?

In this experiment, the flashlight acts like the sun, shining light across space. The larger ball is the Earth, and the smaller ball is the moon. When the moon moves between the Earth and the sun, it blocks some of the sunlight, creating an eclipse. This is similar to what happens during a real solar eclipse in space!

Interesting Fact: Did you know that during a total solar eclipse, the moon perfectly covers the sun, even though the sun is much larger? This is because the sun is also much farther away from Earth than the moon is, making them look similar in size from where we stand!

Why do shadows follow me everywhere?

a) Shadows follow you everywhere because they like to play with you.
b) Shadows follow you everywhere because the ground makes a picture of you as you move.
c) Shadows follow you everywhere because when light shines on you, it makes a dark shape behind you.

Explanation:

Imagine the sun or a light bulb as a big flashlight that shines on everything. When the light hits you, it can't go through you because you're solid, just like how a wall blocks the light. Instead, the light goes *around* you, but the light can't reach where you're standing. This creates a dark shape on the ground or wall behind you, and that's your shadow!

Your shadow is always connected to you because wherever you move, you're still blocking the light in the same way, so the shadow moves with you. It's like your shadow is your buddy, always sticking close to you, but it can only show up when there's light.

When the light is in front of you, your shadow is behind you. When the light is behind you, your shadow is in front of you. So, your shadow is really just a part of you, made by the light, and it follows you everywhere because you're the one blocking the light!

Interesting Fact: Did you know your shadow changes size throughout the day? In the morning and late afternoon, your shadow is long when the sun is low in the sky. But your shadow is much shorter when the sun is high in the sky at noon!

Correct answer: c) Shadows follow you everywhere because when light shines on you, it makes a dark shape behind you.

POP QUIZ

1. What creates your shadow when you're standing outside in the sunlight?

a) The sun shining on you, with light being blocked by your body

b) Clouds moving in the sky

c) The wind blowing around you

2. Why does the sun seem to follow you when you're outside?

a) Because it really is moving with you

b) Because the sun is super far away, so it looks like it's in the same spot no matter where you go

c) Because it's playing a game of hide and seek

3. Why shouldn't you look directly at the sun?

a) Because it's too far away to see clearly

b) Because it's so bright that it can hurt your eyes

c) Because it's not actually in the sky

What items are effective for sun protection?

Correct answer: a, b, b

Why does the moon change shape?

a) The moon changes shape because of how we see the sunlight reflecting off it from Earth.

b) The moon changes shape because it's made of cheese, and space mice nibble on it.

c) The moon changes shape because it's a magical creature that can transform.

Explanation:

Let's imagine you're holding a ball in a dark room, and you have a flashlight. If you shine the flashlight on the ball, one side lights up, right? But what about the side that's not facing the flashlight? It's in the shadow and looks dark. Our moon is a bit like that ball, and the sun is like our flashlight.

The moon doesn't actually change shape; it's always round like a ball. But as it orbits or moves around the Earth, different parts of it are lit up by the sun's light, which makes it look like it's changing shape.

Sometimes, the moon is between the Earth and the sun, and the side of the moon that's lit up by the sun is facing away from us. We can't see the lit-up side, so the moon looks dark. We call this a new moon. As the moon moves around the Earth, more and more of the lit-up side becomes visible to us, until we eventually see the whole lit-up side. That's a full moon.

So, it's not because it's made of cheese or because it's magical. It's all about how sunlight shines on the moon and how we see it from Earth. Isn't that cool?

Interesting Fact: Did you know that it takes about 27.3 days for the moon to orbit around the Earth? That's almost a month! This is why the phases of the moon cycle approximately every month.

Correct Answer: a) The moon changes shape because of how we see the sunlight reflecting off it from Earth.

Can the moon fall down to Earth?

a) Yes, the moon could fall down to Earth if it gets too close.
b) No, the moon can't fall down to Earth because it's held in place by gravity.
c) Maybe, but only if a big rocket pushes it towards Earth.

Explanation:

Imagine you're holding a ball on a string and swinging it around in a circle. The ball keeps going around and around, but it doesn’t fly away or fall because the string is holding it in place. The moon works in a similar way, except instead of a string, the moon is held by something called gravity.

Gravity is a special force that pulls objects toward each other. The Earth's gravity is very strong, pulling the moon toward it like the string holds the ball. But the moon is also moving very fast around the Earth. Instead of falling down, the moon keeps moving in a circle around our planet, like the ball swinging around on the string.

It's like riding a merry-go-round! When you're spinning around, you don't fall off because you're holding on tight, and the spinning keeps you moving in a circle. The moon is "holding on" with gravity, and it's always moving in a circle around Earth, so it doesn't fall down.

This is called **orbiting**. So, the moon is not going to fall to Earth because gravity keeps it safely in its orbit, spinning around our planet, just like the ball stays safely on the string when you swing it.

Interesting Fact: Did you know that the moon is slowly moving away from Earth? Every year, the moon drifts about an inch farther away from us, but it's still close enough to stay in its orbit!

Correct answer: b) No, the moon can't fall down to Earth because it's held in place by gravity.

Can people live on the moon?

a) Yes, people can live on the moon because it has air and water like Earth.

b) No, people can't live on the moon because there's no air to breathe or water to drink.

c) Maybe, but only if they bring their own food and build houses there.

Explanation:

Imagine you're going camping, but you forgot to bring food, water, and a tent. It would be hard to stay there for long, right? Well, living on the moon is kind of like that! The moon doesn't have the things we need to survive, like air to breathe, water to drink, and food to eat. On Earth, we have something called the atmosphere, which is a layer of air that surrounds our planet. The moon doesn't have an atmosphere like Earth does, so there's no oxygen to breathe, which makes it impossible for people to live there without special equipment.

Also, the moon doesn't have rivers, lakes, or oceans like Earth, so there's no water. On top of that, it gets really, really hot during the day and super cold at night on the moon because there's no atmosphere to keep the temperature stable. That would make it tough to live there!

It's kind of like going to the desert without any supplies. You'd need special clothes, air tanks, and lots of gear just to stay safe. That's why astronauts who visit the moon wear spacesuits with oxygen tanks to help them breathe and protect them from the extreme temperatures.

So, while people can visit the moon for a short time, they can't live there like we do on Earth because the moon doesn't have the things we need to survive.

Interesting Fact: Did you know that the footprints left by astronauts on the moon are still there today? Since there's no wind or rain on the moon, they stay exactly the same, even after many years!

Correct answer: b) No, people can't live on the moon because there's no air to breathe or water to drink.

POP QUIZ

1. Why does the moon look like it changes shape?

a) Because different parts of the moon are lit up by the sun as it moves around the Earth

b) Because it's made of cheese

c) Because the moon gets bigger and smaller every night

2. Why do astronauts wear special suits on the moon?

a) To look cool

b) To keep their clothes clean

c) To protect themselves from the extreme temperatures and lack of air

3. What makes the moon orbit around the Earth?

a) A giant magnet in the sky

b) Gravity, which pulls the moon around the Earth

c) The moon's engine

Guide Luna the Mouse to Her Moon Cheese!

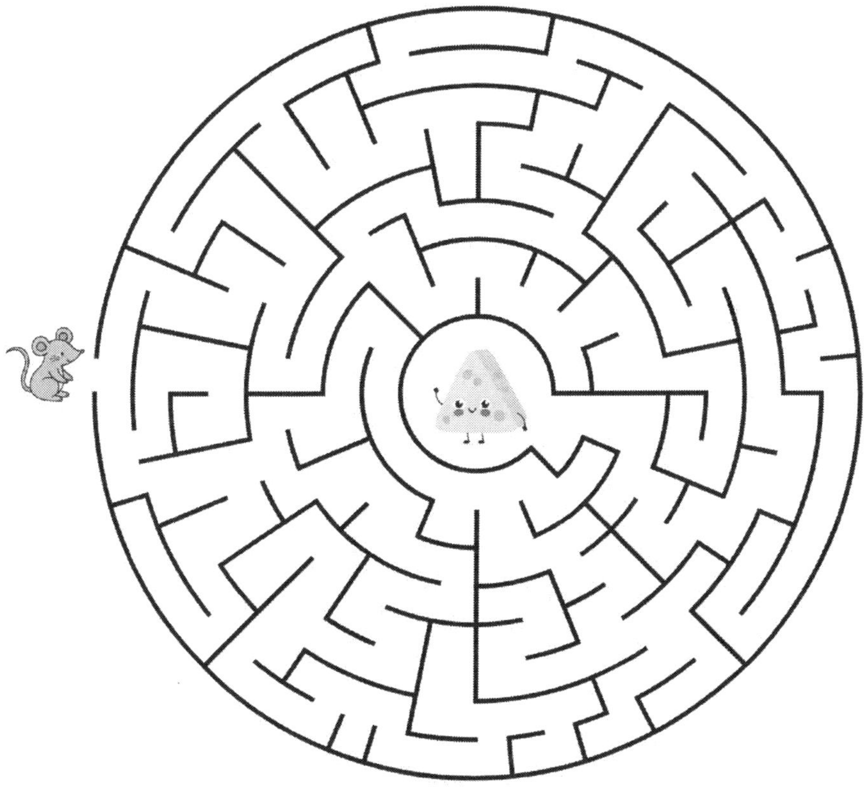

Correct answer: a, c, b

How do stars get up in the sky at night?

a) Stars get up in the sky at night because they wake up when the sun goes to sleep.
b) Stars are placed in the sky every night by invisible fairies.
c) Stars are always in the sky, but we can only see them at night when the sky is dark.

Explanation:

During the day, the sun is so bright that it lights up the whole sky, making it hard for us to see the stars. But the stars don't go away; they're still up there, shining in space. When the sun sets, and the sky gets dark, the stars become easier to see, like tiny twinkling lights.

Imagine you have a flashlight and you turn it on during the day. It's really hard to see the light because everything around you is already so bright, right? But if you turn the flashlight on at night, when everything is dark, it shines brightly and you can see it much better. The stars in the sky are like that. They are always there, but during the daytime, the sun's bright light makes it hard for us to see them.

The stars don't disappear during the day or fly into the sky at night. They stay in the same place, far, far away in space. The reason we see them at night is because the sun goes down, and the sky gets dark. Without the sun's bright light, the stars become visible, just like how your flashlight is easier to see when it's dark outside.

So, the stars are always up there in the sky, waiting to shine brightly once the sun sets!

Interesting Fact: Did you know that some of the stars you see at night are so far away that their light takes millions of years to reach us? That means when you look at the stars, you're seeing light that started its journey a long, long time ago!

Correct answer: c) Stars are always in the sky, but we can only see them at night when the sky is dark.

Why do stars twinkle?

a) Stars twinkle because their light passes through Earth's atmosphere, which makes it look like they are blinking.
b) Stars twinkle because they are moving around in space.
c) Stars twinkle because they are turning on and off like lights.

Explanation:

Stars are very far away from us, and their light travels a long distance to reach Earth. On its way, the light has to pass through Earth's atmosphere, which is full of moving air. The air in our atmosphere is always moving and changing because of wind, temperature, and other weather conditions.

When the starlight passes through the moving air, it bends and bounces in different directions. This bending of light is called refraction. Because the air is always moving, the light keeps changing direction, making the star's light look like it's twinkling or blinking.

Imagine you are looking at a streetlight through a glass of water. The light might look wobbly or like it's changing colour. This happens because the water bends the light in different ways as it moves. The same thing happens when you look at stars in the night sky.

So, stars don't really twinkle on their own. They shine steadily, but the Earth's atmosphere makes their light look like it's flickering. In short, stars twinkle because their light passes through Earth's atmosphere, which bends the light and makes it look like the stars are blinking. This is why we see stars twinkling when we look up at the night sky!

Interesting Fact: Did you know that stars don't twinkle when they're viewed from outer space? That's because there's no atmosphere to refract their light. Astronauts who look at stars from space see them as steady points of light, not twinkling stars!

Correct answer: a) Stars twinkle because their light passes through Earth's atmosphere, which makes it look like they are blinking.

Bonus Experiment: Why Do Stars Twinkle?

Objective: To help understand why stars twinkle by creating a simple model that mimics the effect.

What You'll Need:

- A flashlight or small LED light
- A clear glass of water
- A pen
- A piece of aluminium foil
- A dark room or a space where you can dim the lights

Steps:

1. Set Up the Star: Pierce several small holes in a piece of aluminium foil using a pen. This represents stars. Place the foil in front of a torch (flashlight) and make sure the light shines through the holes, representing twinkling stars.

2. Prepare the Atmosphere: Fill a bowl with water and add a few drops of dish soap or milk to make the water slightly cloudy. This cloudy water acts like Earth's atmosphere, which bends light and causes stars to appear to twinkle.

3. Observe the Twinkling: Dim the lights in the room. Shine the torch through the aluminium foil so the light passes through the cloudy water before reaching your eyes. Observe how the light appears to flicker or twinkle, just like stars in the night sky.

What's Happening?

This experiment shows why stars appear to twinkle. The cloudy water represents the Earth's atmosphere, which is full of moving air and tiny particles. As the light from the "star" passes through the atmosphere, it gets bent and scattered in different directions. This bending and scattering make the star's light appear to flicker or twinkle when we see it from Earth.

Why does meteor shower happen?

a) Meteor showers happen when Earth passes through a trail of dust and rocks left by a comet.
b) Meteor showers happen because the moon pulls pieces of the sky down with its gravity.
c) Meteor showers happen because the moon is having a night-time disco party, and the stars are dancing too hard, throwing glitter everywhere!

Explanation:

Imagine you're riding your bike through a pile of leaves on the ground. As you go through the leaves, they get kicked up into the air and swirl around you. That's kind of like what happens during a meteor shower! But instead of leaves, Earth is moving through space, and it passes through a trail of dust and tiny rocks that were left behind by a comet.

Comets are like big, dirty snowballs in space that travel around the sun. As a comet gets close to the sun, it starts to melt a little, leaving behind a trail of tiny dust and rocks. This trail stays in space, floating around, even after the comet moves away.

As Earth moves around the sun, sometimes it goes through one of these trails of dust and rocks. When that happens, the tiny pieces from the comet enter Earth's atmosphere (the layer of air around our planet) and start to burn up. When they burn up, they create bright streaks of light in the sky that we call meteors. If lots of these meteors happen at once, it's called a meteor shower!

So, meteor showers are like a light show in the sky made by tiny pieces of space dust and rocks. It's really cool to watch, but don't worry—those meteors are so small that they burn up completely before they can reach the ground.

Interesting Fact: Did you know that during a meteor shower, you might see over 100 meteors in just one hour if the conditions are right? It's like a natural fireworks show in the sky!

Correct Answer: b) Meteor showers happen when Earth passes through a trail of dust and rocks left by a comet.

POP QUIZ

1. Why can't we see stars during the day?

a) They turn off like lights

b) The sun's brightness makes it hard to see them

c) They hide behind clouds

2. What makes stars twinkle at night?

a) The stars are blinking on and off

b) The stars are moving quickly

c) The Earth's atmosphere bends the starlight as it passes through

3. Why do stars seem to come out when the sun goes down?

a) They were sleeping during the day

b) Their work shift is only at night

c) The sky gets dark, so we can see their steady light better

Escape the star maze

Correct answer: b, c, c

Why does it rain?

a) It rains because the sky is crying.
b) It rains because water vapor in the air cools down, condenses into droplets, and falls to the ground.
c) It rains because the wind blows water from the oceans into the clouds.

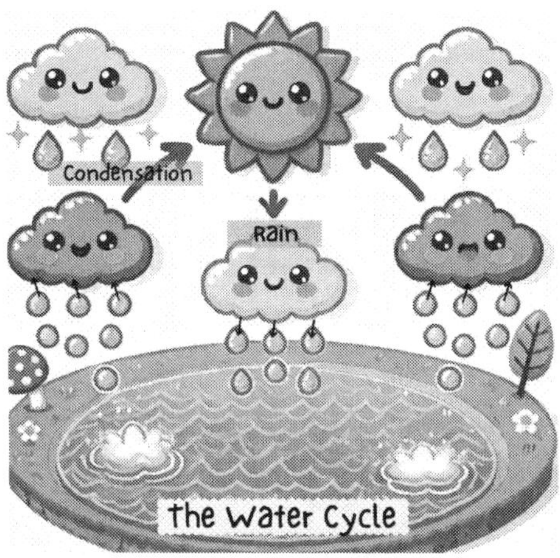

Explanation:

Think about when you boil water in a pot. You see steam rising from the water. This steam is water vapor, which is water in its gas form. In nature, the sun heats up water in oceans, lakes, and rivers, turning it into water vapor. This water vapor rises into the sky and mixes with the air.

As the water vapor rises higher in the sky, it cools down. When the water vapor cools, it turns back into tiny water droplets, just like when steam from a hot shower turns into droplets on a mirror. This process is called **condensation**.

These tiny water droplets come together to form clouds. When many droplets join together, they get heavier and heavier. When they become too heavy to stay in the cloud, they fall to the ground as rain.

Imagine you have a sponge full of water. When the sponge gets too full, water starts to drip out. The clouds are like sponges, and the water droplets are like the water in the sponge. When the clouds can't hold any more water, it rains!

So, it rains because water vapor in the air cools down, condenses into droplets, and falls to the ground. This process is part of *the water cycle*, which is how water moves from the ground to the sky and back again. Rain helps plants grow, fills up rivers and lakes, and keeps everything alive. It's an important part of how nature works!

Interesting Fact: Did you know that raindrops are not tear-shaped like they're often drawn in pictures? They're actually shaped like tiny hamburger buns!

Correct Answer: b) It rains because water vapor in the air cools down, condenses into droplets, and falls to the ground.

Bonus Experiment: Make It Rain in a Jar

What You'll Need:

- A large clear glass jar
- Hot water (ask an adult for help!)
- Ice cubes
- A plate or lid that can cover the top of the jar
- A small plastic bag or ziplock bag filled with ice cubes (optional)

Steps:

1. Fill the Jar: With the help of an adult, pour about 1-2 inches of hot water into the jar. The water should be steaming but not boiling.

2. Cover the Jar: Quickly place the plate or lid on top of the jar. This traps the warm, moist air inside the jar.

3. Add the Ice: Place the ice cubes on top of the plate or lid. You can also use a plastic bag filled with ice cubes for less mess.

4. Watch It Rain: After a few minutes, look inside the jar. You should see small water droplets forming on the inside of the jar and then "rain" falling from the lid to the bottom of the jar.

What's Happening?

This experiment shows how rain is made. The hot water creates warm, moist air inside the jar. When the warm air rises and touches the cold lid, it cools down, and the water vapor turns into tiny water droplets, just like how clouds form in the sky. As more droplets form, they get heavier and fall down as "rain."

Why does the sky make thunder and lightning?

a) The sky makes thunder and lightning because stars are falling from space.
b) The sky produces thunder and lightning when it is upset about something.
c) The sky makes thunder and lightning when ice and water inside clouds collide, creating electric charges.

Explanation:

Think of the sky as a big, magical place where electricity can form inside clouds. Sometimes, when the clouds get really full of this electricity, it releases in a big, bright flash called lightning.

Imagine you're rubbing a balloon on your hair. After a while, you notice your hair sticks to the balloon and little sparks of electricity may even appear. That's because you created something called

static electricity. The clouds in the sky do something similar during a thunderstorm!

When big, dark storm clouds move around, they rub against each other, creating something like that static electricity you made with the balloon. Inside the clouds are tiny particles like ice and water droplets that bump into each other, building up electricity. After a while, so much electricity builds up that it has to be released somehow. That's when you see lightning like a giant spark in the sky!

Lightning is super powerful and very hot, and it moves really fast! It heats the air around it very quickly. When the air gets heated up, it expands and then crashes together, making a loud boom called thunder.

It's like popping a balloon—the sudden burst makes a loud noise, and in the case of lightning, that noise is thunder! Lightning and thunder happen almost at the same time, but since light travels faster than sound, we usually see the lightning first and hear the thunder a little later.

Interesting Fact: Did you know that lightning can be hotter than the surface of the Sun? In fact, a single bolt of lightning can reach temperatures of up to 30,000 degrees Celsius (54,000 degrees Fahrenheit)!

Correct answer: c) The sky makes thunder and lightning when ice and water inside clouds collide, creating electric charges.

Science Observation Experiment: Thunder and Lightning

Objective: To understand the relationship between thunder and lightning by observing and recording their observations during a storm.

What You'll Need:

- A notebook or paper
- A pencil or pen
- A clock or stopwatch
- A safe place indoors with a window view of the sky (like your living room or a covered porch)

Important! This experiment should only be done with an adult present and from a safe indoor location. Never go outside during a thunderstorm!

Steps:

1. **Get Ready:** Find a comfortable and safe spot indoors where you can see the sky. Bring your notebook and pencil with you. Make sure you can see out the window, but stay away from the glass.

2. **Listen and Watch:** When you see a flash of lightning, start counting the seconds (you can say "one Mississippi, two Mississippi" to keep track). Keep counting until you hear the thunder.

3. Record Your Observations: In your notebook, write down how many seconds passed between the lightning and the thunder. Do this each time you see lightning and hear thunder during the storm.

4. Repeat: Try to observe several flashes of lightning and thunderclaps. Write down your results for each one.

What's Happening?

Lightning and thunder happen at the same time, but light travels much faster than sound. That's why we see the lightning before we hear the thunder. By counting the seconds between the lightning and the thunder, you can estimate how far away the storm is. Every 5 seconds between the flash and the thunder means the storm is about 1 mile (or 1.6 kilometers) away.

Safety Note: Always stay indoors during a thunderstorm. Lightning is very dangerous, so it's important to stay safe while you observe.

POP QUIZ

1. What causes the loud noise called thunder during a storm?

a) Clouds bumping into each other

b) The fast movement of air after lightning heats it up

c) Rain hitting the ground

2. Why does lightning happen in the sky?

a) Because clouds are full of electricity and let it go in a big, bright flash

b) Because the Sun is too hot

c) Because the air is full of steam

3. Why does the sky rain?

a) Because the clouds are tired

b) Because the Sun shines too brightly

c) Because water droplets in the clouds get too heavy and fall to the ground

Word Search

S	G	A	S	T	R	O	N	A	U	T	E	S
H	K	U	T	M	Y	D	O	E	C	R	A	I
O	R	O	E	N	K	I	F	H	T	A	R	N
O	A	S	C	L	O	U	D	U	W	I	L	S
T	E	T	H	U	N	D	E	R	I	N	I	P
I	S	R	M	O	O	N	M	K	N	B	G	A
N	O	U	F	L	B	R	E	A	K	O	H	C
G	H	U	N	O	T	E	S	R	L	W	T	E
S	H	W	B	I	N	E	T	T	E	L	N	A
T	P	H	I	I	S	E	T	O	A	R	I	V
A	A	C	A	N	K	P	T	H	D	R	N	S
R	A	R	O	B	Y	H	M	C	S	G	G	I
S	H	A	D	O	W	A	W	T	O	N	U	H
M	E	T	E	O	R	S	H	O	W	E	R	L

ASTRONAUT
CLOUD
LIGHTNING
METEOR SHOWER
MOON
RAIN
RAINBOW
SHADOW
SHOOTING STAR
SKY
SPACE
STAR
SUN
THUNDER
TWINKLE

Answer: b, a, c

A BIG Thank You!

We hope you and your little ones have been loving ***The Ultimate WHY Book***! We're all about answering those big "WHY" questions that kids seem to ask a million times a day, and we know that curiosity is a gift. But guess what? By leaving a review, you're not just helping us – you're helping so many other curious kids and their grown-ups discover the wonders of nature too!

So here's a question for you:

Have you ever found something amazing – like a great recipe or a super fun game – and felt that warm fuzzy feeling when you share it with a friend? That's exactly what you're doing when you leave a review. You're giving other families the chance to dive into a book that might just spark a lifelong love of learning and exploration in their kids.

> **Leaving a review for *The Ultimate WHY Book* is like putting a little extra magic into the world.**

It's an opportunity to share your thoughts and experiences with other parents, caregivers, and kids who are just waiting to find their next favorite book. Imagine a child somewhere out there who's been asking "Why is the sky blue?" and is just itching for a fun, easy-to-understand explanation. Your review might be the nudge their parent needs to pick up this book and say, "Aha! Here's the answer!"

Now, we know your time is valuable (you've probably got a lot of WHY questions on your hands right now!), but by leaving a quick review, you'll be helping other families find a book that's packed with playful analogies, adorable pictures, and fun mini-experiments that make learning science super exciting. Your honest feedback will also help us improve, so we can keep creating books that inspire the next generation of scientists, thinkers, and dreamers.

How do you leave a review? We've made it super simple! Just scan the QR code below, and it'll take you directly to our review page. All you need to do is share your thoughts – it can be as simple or as detailed as you'd like. A few sentences can go a long way in helping others discover the fun inside *The Ultimate WHY Book*.

Your review makes a difference. When parents see real experiences from people like you, it helps them make decisions about what books to share with their kids. Reviews help us reach more families who are looking for a fun way to answer life's big questions, and they can inspire kids all over the world to stay curious about the world around them.

As a thank you, think about the joy you'll be spreading – not just to other parents, but to the kiddos who will soon be saying, "Wow!

That's why the sky is blue!" You're introducing them to a world of discovery, and that's a gift that will keep on giving. Plus, in the world of writing and publishing, your support helps us grow and keeps us motivated to continue creating more awesome content for curious minds everywhere.

So, what do you say? Will you take a moment to leave a review and share the magic? We're excited to hear your thoughts, and we know others will be too. Just scan the QR code above to get started.

Thank you so much for being part of our curious community!

Happy learning and exploring!

Answers

Page 17 - 16 clouds

Page 43

Page 51

Page 61

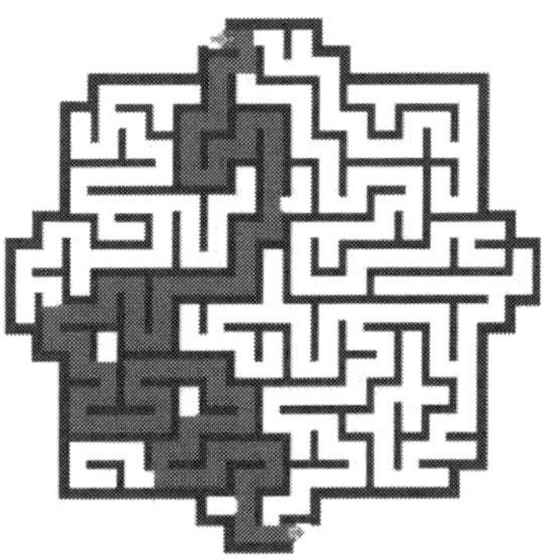

Page 71

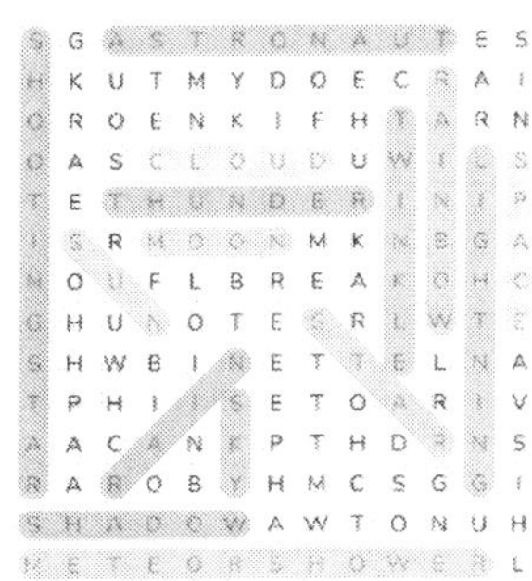

References

Admin. (2022, May 31). Why doesn't the moon fall into the Earth? - CBSE Class 6-10. BYJUS. https://byjus.com/physics/why-doesnt-the-moon-fall-into-the-earth/

Ask an astronomer. (n.d.). Cool Cosmos. https://coolcosmos.ipac.caltech.edu/ask/210-Why-do-the-stars-twinkle

Clouds and precipitation weather: How do clouds form? (n.d.). Slideplayer. http://slideplayer.com/slide/5981283/

Danielle. (2023, April 18). Make a cloud form in a jar science experiment. Cool Science Experiments Headquarters. https://coolscienceexperimentshq.com/make-a-cloud-form-in-a-jar/

Earth's atmosphere: A multi-layered cake. (n.d.). NASA Science. https://science.nasa.gov/earth/earth-atmosphere/earths-atmosphere-a-multi-layered-cake/

Education, U. C. F. S. (n.d.). The colors of the sky. UCAR. https://scied.ucar.edu/kids/sky-wonders/colors-sky

Facts about the moon. (n.d.). Actforlibraries.org. http://www.actforlibraries.org/facts-about-the-moon-10/

Hiskey, D. (2013, June 21). Why the sky is blue. Today I Found Out. https://www.todayifoundout.com/index.php/2010/05/why-the-sky-is-blue/

How to explain the water cycle. (n.d.). Star Language Blog. https://www.starlanguageblog.com/how-to-explain-the-water-cycle/

Immelman, M. (2023, September 3). 5 easy science experiments for kids. Kidsgearguide. https://www.kidsgearguide.com/5-easy-science-experiments-for-kids/

Living on the moon: How to make it possible. (n.d.). HeroX. https://www.herox.com/blog/957-3-problems-we-need-to-solve-before-we-can-live-on

Marcy, A. (2024, April 12). Make sky in a jar! Double Helix. https://blog.doublehelix.csiro.au/make-sky-in-a-jar/

Ochoa, C. (2023, January 11). How to make a rainbow with an experiment and craft. Little Passports. https://www.littlepassports.com/blog/craft-diy/how-to-make-a-rainbow/

Popardowski, E., Hebda, T., & Jakubowski, T. (2022). The effect of UV-C irradiation on the mechanical and physiological properties of potato tuber and different products. *Applied Sciences, 12*(12), 5907.

Quora. (2017, June 15). Why can't we see stars during the day? *Forbes.* https://www.forbes.com/sites/quora/2017/06/15/why-cant-we-see-stars-during-the-day/

Rainbow. (n.d.). Ilmiosito. https://www.isabellafabbri.com/rainbow

Refraction of light. (n.d.). Science Learning Hub. https://www.sciencelearn.org.nz/resources/49-refraction-of-light

Saunders, T. (n.d.). How hot is the sun? Our star's staggering temperature, explained. *BBC Science Focus Magazine.* https://www.sciencefocus.com/space/how-hot-is-the-sun/

Shooting star craft. (n.d.). Twinkl. https://www.twinkl.com.au/resource/paper-plate-shooting-star-space-crafts-t-tc-1664305795

Stars. (n.d.). NASA Science. https://science.nasa.gov/universe/stars/

The color of clouds. (n.d.). National Oceanic and Atmospheric Administration. https://www.noaa.gov/jetstream/clouds/color-of-clouds

The science behind why the sky appears blue: Explained. (n.d.). Factober. https://factober.com/article/the-science-behind-why-the-sky-appears-blue-explained/

The water cycle steps: How the water cycle works step by step. (n.d.). Smartclass4kids. https://smartclass4kids.com/the-water-cycle/

Theick. (2023, August 31). Why is the sky blue? LearnThought. https://learnthought.com/science/why-is-the-sky-blue/

Thoopal, R. K. (2005, August 18). Why does the sun follow you? Pitara Kids Network. https://www.pitara.com/science-for-kids/5ws-and-h/why-does-the-sun-follow-you/

Toppr. (2022, September 5). During scattering of light: The amount of scattering is inversely proportional to the wavelength of light. Toppr Ask. https://www.toppr.com/ask/en-au/question/during-scattering-of-light-the-amount-of-scattering-is-inversely/

Water cycle. (n.d.). BrainKart. https://www.brainkart.com/article/Water-cycle_43134/

What is a solar eclipse? (n.d.). NASA Space Place. https://spaceplace.nasa.gov/eclipse-snap/en/

Why can't you look directly at the sun? (2018, May 16). Wonderopolis. https://www.wonderopolis.org/wonder/why-cant-you-look-directly-at-the-sun/

Why do stars twinkle? (n.d.). Nanogirl. https://www.nanogirl.co/science-experiments-videos/why-do-stars-twinkle/

Why is the sky blue? (n.d.). NASA Space Place. https://spaceplace.nasa.gov/blue-sky/en/

Made in the USA
Las Vegas, NV
02 March 2026

42951189R00048